This book contains original reproducible journ copyrights.

The original purchaser of this book is authorized to reproduce and use the individual items in this book for the generation of creative activity in the psychiatric/therapeutic/ educational setting. However, the reproducible journal page collection in this book may not be reprinted in whole or in part as a reproducible handout book collection, or for any other purpose without the written permission of the author.

This publication is sold with the understanding that the publisher is not engaged in rendering psychological, medical, or other professional services.

Dear Reader,

The process of grieving can be a long and complicated one. It is different for everyone, but never easy. This journal is designed to help you work through some of the issues associated with grief. You should do only the pages you feel ready for and those that apply to you. You can always come back later for the sections you pass over. Feel free to share your writings with someone you trust, or keep it private if you prefer. There are no page numbers and no lines so use this journal however you wish. You can draw pictures, write poetry, or simply write your thoughts.

The Author

This is who you were

This is what you meant to me

I never thought I would lose you

This is the story of how you died

I was so angry when you died

I did things I wish I hadn't as a result

....

I did things I wish I hadn't as a result

Sometimes I feel like it was my fault

Sometimes I feel overwhelmed

I'm afraid

I just want to be alone

I have pushed friends and family away as a result

My friends/family don't understand

I'm lonely

I worry now about other loved ones

I have had thoughts of hurting myself

I wish I had told you

I feel guilty

These things remind me of you

It's hard for me to focus on things

School is different now

Some days are harder than others

I'm putting a lot of pressure on myself to be perfect

I'm putting a lot of pressure on myself to be perfect

I wish

I hope

I need

This has helped me with my grief

I wrote/drew this about you

You believed in me

My faith has helped me

You taught me

My happiest memories of our time together

Sometimes I feel you looking over me

This is how I honor your memory

I am trying to rebuild my life now that you are no longer in it.

This is who I can talk to about you

I've had dreams about you

I will never forget you

Thoughts...

Made in the USA
Columbia, SC
20 December 2021

52258982R00024